I AM A ~~MAD~~ *Magnificent* ASIAN MOM

POSITIVE AFFIRMATION FOR ASIAN AMERICAN MOMS

BY YOBE QIU

ILLUSTRATED BY KITTY WONG

I AM A

Modern

ASIAN MOM.

I HONOR THE GENERATIONS THAT PAVED THE WAY.
LIVING MY ANCESTORS' WILDEST DREAMS, THEY SAY!

THERE'S NOTHING I CAN'T DO.
I CAN ACHIEVE EVERYTHING
THAT I PUT MY MIND TO!

I AM A

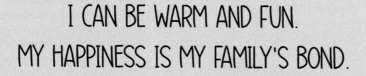

ASIAN MOM.

I CAN BE WARM AND FUN.
MY HAPPINESS IS MY FAMILY'S BOND.

I SAY NO TO TOXICITY,
I TAKE CONTROL OF HOW I RESPOND.

I AM A *Majestic* ASIAN MOM.

MY HEIGHT AND MY EYES LOOK BEST ON ME;
MY SKIN AND MY HAIR MAKE THEM SAY O.M.G.

THIS FIGURE, THESE CURVES,
THESE LIPS ARE THE BOMB;
I LOOK EXACTLY HOW I WANT TO,
I DESERVE THE CROWN.

I AM A Marvelous ASIAN MOM.

I DON'T NEED TO PROVE THAT I CAN DO IT ALL;
I DESERVE THE TIME TO REWIND.

I CAN INDULGE A HOT BOWL OF PHỞ,
AND ALSO ENJOY THAT
FULL GLASS OF WINE.

I AM A
Multi-talented
ASIAN MOM.

FROM CLOSING DEALS TO FEEDING MY BABY,
I CAN HANDLE IT ALL, THERE IS NO MAYBE!

UNSOLICITED ADVICE, I CAN TUNE THEM OUT.
DON'T TEST ME,
I'M THAT LADY!

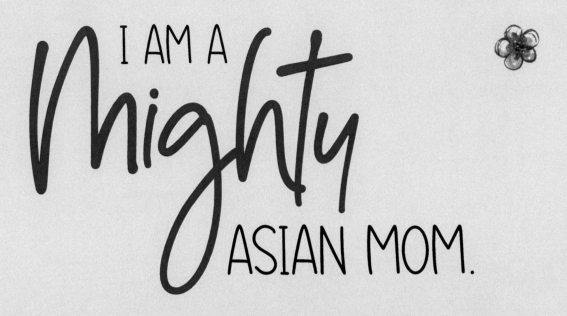

I AM A

Mighty

ASIAN MOM.

STRONG, INDEPENDENT, DETERMINED, AND FILLED WITH PRIDE.
I CAN RAISE BABIES AND START A BUSINESS ON THE SIDE!

I'M UNWAVERING LIKE A MOUNTAIN,
BOTH ON THE OUTSIDE AND THE INSIDE.

I AM A *Mindful* ASIAN MOM.

I AM PROUD OF MY IDENTITY AND MY CULTURE TOO.
I EMBRACE MY TRADITIONS IN EVERYTHING I DO.

I MAKE IT MY GOAL –
TO BE HAPPY AND FULFILLED,
IN MY BODY AND MY SOUL!

I AM A
Motivated
ASIAN MOM.

LIFE IS NOT FAIR, BUT I'VE TRIED;
I CAN HANDLE ANYTHING I WANT TO DO.

BREAKING BAMBOO CEILINGS AT WORK,
AND RESETTING GENDER ROLES AT HOME, TOO.

I AM A

Memorable

ASIAN MOM.

I DON'T MIND STANDING OUT FROM THE CROWD,
I AM UNFORGETTABLE, QUIET OR LOUD.

I WILL CONTINUE TO SURPRISE MYSELF,
FOR HOW MUCH I'VE EXCELLED,
AFTER HOW HARD I FELL.

I AM A Miraculous ASIAN MOM.

THE TIMES CAN BE DIFFICULT,
BUT I AM A F*CKING MIRACLE!

THERE'S NO ONE ELSE LIKE ME,
I AM WHO I WANT TO BE –
YESTERDAY, TODAY, AND TOMORROW.

I AM MODERN, MERRY, MAJESTIC, MARVELOUS,
MULTI-TALENTED, MIGHTY, MINDFUL, MOTIVATED,
MEMORABLE, MIRACULOUS, AND SO MUCH MORE!

I AM A

Magnificent

ASIAN MOM,

THAT I KNOW FOR SURE!

ABOUT THE AUTHOR:

Yobe Qiu is an educator, entrepreneur, mom, and bestselling author with a passion for storytelling. As an educator, Yobe taught children and their families to embrace love and diverse cultures. When she identified a need for more multicultural books, she decided to create her own children's stories featuring Asian characters and cultures. Today, Yobe is proud to publish books that help children like her daughters and mom friends feel seen, heard, and represented. Yobe lives in New Jersey with her daughters and husband!

For school, corporate and non-profit organizations events and bulk orders,
please contact Yobe's team at hello@byyobeqiu.com

DEDICATION:

Mom,

Thank you for being our rock, our inspiration, the glue that holds our family together. You are the strongest person I know with the biggest heart. Thanks for being a fantastic role model for all of us!

– Love, Ida

All inquiries including bulk purchase for promotional, educational, and business events, should be directed to hello@byyobeqiu.com.

Illustrated by Kitty Wong
Edited and designed by Duck Duck Books

Published by By Yobe Qiu, Inc 2023